DIGITAL AND INFORMATION LITERACY ™

BUILDING APPS

LAURA LA BELLA

rosen publishing's

rosen central®

New York

Published in 2014 by The Rosen Publishing Group, Inc.
29 East 21st Street, New York, NY 10010

Library of Congress Cataloging-in-Publication Data

La Bella, Laura.
Building apps/Laura La Bella. — 1st ed. — New York : Rosen, c2014
    p. cm. — (Digital and information literacy)
Includes bibliographical references and index.
ISBN 978-1-4488-9515-1 (library binding)
1. Computer programming—Juvenile literature. 2. Application software—Development.
I. Title.
QA76.76.D47 .L3 2014
005.1

Manufactured in the United States of America

CPSIA Compliance Information: Batch #S13YA: For further information, contact Rosen Publishing, New York, New York, at 1-800-237-9932.

CONTENTS

INTRODUCTION

It seems there is an app for literally every need, big and small. There are apps to help you do pretty much everything these days, from navigating road trips, finding food and hotels, and getting weather updates and sports scores to hanging level photos on your walls and managing your money. The list of different types of apps can go on and on.

Why are there so many apps? With the popularity of smartphones and tablet computers, apps let you access information quickly, from virtually anywhere, at the touch of a button. And with new apps being launched every day, there is no shortage of developers who have a great idea for the next big app.

Building apps can be a fun, exciting thing to do. But behind the scenes, there is serious and hard work taking place by developers who have the skills to take an idea and turn it into an app. There are several different kinds of devices to create apps for, such as smartphones and tablets that run on Apple and Android operating systems. For this reason, creating an app that will stand out from the crowd and somehow attract the attention of a lot of customers isn't as easy as it sounds. But the reward when you create a popular app is incredibly exciting and fulfilling. And it can lead to even greater opportunities and success in app design and development!

Nick D'Aloisio, sixteen, of Great Britain, invented an iPhone app called Summly, which condenses the text of long Web pages into bullet points for easy reading. D'Aloisio is one of a number of teens who have invented apps for smartphones.

Chapter 1

What Are Apps?

Short for application software, an "app" is designed to help a user perform a task. Apps help with everything from seeking academic assistance, playing games, and getting driving directions to obtaining weather updates, recipes, and sports scores. All of this information and assistance is accessed and delivered via a smartphone or tablet computer.

Apps can help a user gather information for school or work, or they can be used for fun and entertainment. For example, Star Walk lets a user hold his or her phone up to the sky, and the app will then highlight constellations and planets based on where the user is standing. For a science class, this app can help students improve their understanding of astronomy. It can also enable teachers to provide a guided tour of the solar system and the local night sky.

In contrast, fun and entertaining apps, like Shazam Encore, can recognize almost any song that is playing on the radio or over a store's or restaurant's speaker system. The app will automatically provide the user with the song title and artist information. Shazam Encore also lets users buy the song immediately or tag it for download at a later date. It's now possible to find an app for any need, deliberate or random, serious or fun, educational or merely entertaining.

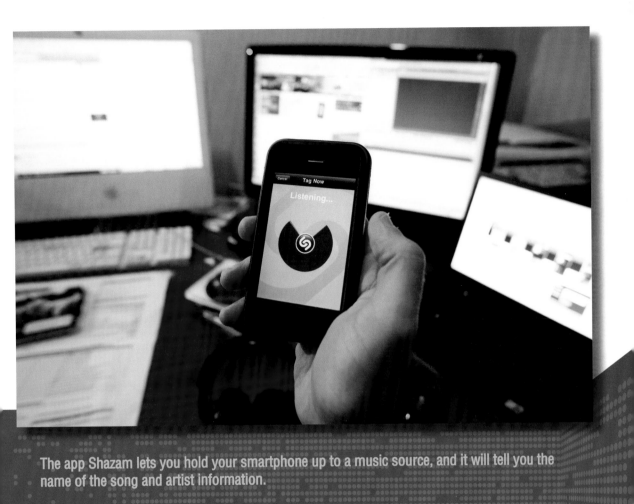

The app Shazam lets you hold your smartphone up to a music source, and it will tell you the name of the song and artist information.

How Smartphones Changed the World

When Apple introduced the iPhone and launched its App Store in 2008, an explosion of app development took place. The iPhone debuted a superior user interface that was unavailable on other mobile phones. It also enabled users to buy apps via iTunes, an integrated purchasing system that lets users download a wide variety of songs and apps.

ITunes pulled the distribution of apps away from mobile phone carriers like AT&T and Verizon (which provide calling capability and Internet connection).

Smartphones have enabled people to get access to countless types of information, from news and weather reports to up-to-the-minute sports scores. Smartphones also have become essential tools for daily living. They can provide directions and navigation and even help you locate restaurants and gas stations when traveling.

Instead, it put it in the hands of stores like the Apple App Store, which sold a huge number of apps to iPhone customers directly. This change also allowed app developers more freedom in creating apps for different uses and selling them directly to customers. Smartphones became a general platform for running apps developed by third-party designers (those not employed by Apple and other smartphone manufacturers).

A few years ago, mobile phones were sold with preset features. Now, with apps, users can customize their phone to suit their personal preferences. A sports lover can download sports-related apps, like Yahoo! Fantasy Football, NCAA March Madness on Demand, and Watch ESPN. A music lover can populate his or her device with Pandora, PocketGuitar, and Mixmeister Scratch. While everyone who buys an iPhone or Droid X phone purchases the same hardware, each device can now be tailored to the user's liking.

Web Apps

There are two kinds of apps, Web apps and native apps. A Web app, also called a mobile app or mobile Web site, is accessed by users over a network, such as the Internet. Web apps connect users to a Web site, and all or parts of the software are launched from that site each time it is opened.

A Web app is basically a Web site that has been designed for viewing on a mobile device. Appearing on the smaller screens of mobile devices, Web apps are designed to provide only the necessary content a user needs, rather than the full range of content that is available on a traditional Web site and viewed on a laptop or desktop home computer. Web apps are accessible from all Web-enabled mobile devices and can run on almost any platform. This includes smartphones (iPhone or Droid X), tablets (iPad, Samsung Galaxy), and e-reader devices (Kindle Fire, Nexus) that have a compliant Web browser.

Web apps have many advantages. Because Web apps are browser-based, meaning they do not require you to install software, users can launch apps at any time and have instantaneous and automatic access to the latest

It isn't just smartphones that have become useful tools for work and play. Tablets, including the iPad and the Samsung Galaxy Note *(above)*, have impacted how and where we access information and entertainment and how we produce our own creative content.

versions. There is no need to download upgrades. The use of browser-based apps also means that software doesn't take up space on your smartphone or tablet computer, leaving valuable memory for other uses. There are no legacy issues with older software, which might require you to purchase upgrades when new services or capabilities become available. Web apps will update immediately and seamlessly. There are no old versions to clutter your device or accidentally download. Web apps also have no viruses.

File   Edit   View   Favorites   Tools   Help

THERE'S AN APP FOR THAT!

There's an App for That!

With over one million apps available for download, and more being developed and launched on a daily basis, a user can find an app for pretty much any need, task, or activity:

- Are you hanging a photo on the wall and need a level? Download Handy iLevel.
- The next time the lights go out and you're stuck in the dark, if you've downloaded Torch, you'll be able to light your way.
- Do you find yourself in a foreign country and in need of help to translate signage? Word Lens will translate signs in a foreign language once you snap a photo of the sign with your camera phone.
- Looking for a full-length movie to watch on your phone? Crackle can help.

Native Apps

Specifically designed to run on a device's operating system, native apps work only on the platform for which they were built. For example, apps for the iPhone will not work on an Android-based smartphone, such as the Droid X. While native apps take longer and are more costly to build than Web apps, the current technology makes them a superior experience for the user.

Native apps are installed directly within the operating system of the device. For example, Camera+ is a native app that works with the built-in camera of the iPhone or iPad. It was designed to make editing photos quick and easy. When Camera+ is downloaded, it works directly within the operating system of your iPhone or iPad and with the device's camera to enable the user to edit photos. By contrast, because Web apps cannot be installed into an operating system, there cannot be a Web app version of Camera+ to connect with your device's camera.

Most apps are designed as native apps. Native apps have a smoother look and feel and have more polish than Web apps. When it comes to aesthetics and overall user experience, it's difficult for Web apps to outdo native apps.

Apple's iPad can shoot video, take photos, play music, and perform online functions such as Web browsing and e-mail. By downloading apps, the iPad can be used to play games, provide GPS navigation, and find information.

Apps, Apps, and More Apps

Just how many apps are there? At last count, there were more than one-and-a-half million apps available for download, with more being launched each day. Apps are currently available from four places: the Apple App Store, for Apple products; Google Play, for devices that use the Android operating system; Windows Phone Store, for devices that use the Windows operating system; and BlackBerry App World, for Blackberry products.

Users select which store to shop in based on the type of device they own. For example, users of Apple products, such as the iPhone, iPad, and iPod Touch, can only download apps from the Apple Store. Apps for phones and tablets that use the Android operating system can only be found at Google Play.

Chapter 2

So You Want to Build an App?

Deciding to build an app can be exciting. But it takes time, patience, and hard work. And you need a great idea. If you have no interest in gaming, you won't find yourself creating the next *Angry Birds* or *World of Warcraft*. You need to think about what interests you.

What are your hobbies or interests? Think about how a smartphone or tablet can help you track, share, or explore that interest. How will the app work, who will use it, and why? And before you even begin to think about the development stage, you need to define your app, choose your platform, and select the software you will use to create your app.

Defining Your App

With more than a million apps already available, developers face the challenge of making their app different, new, unique, and attention-getting. Before you begin developing your app, it's smart to find out who your competition is.

Since Apple introduced the iPad, competitors have flooded the market with tablet computers, including the Sony Tablet S *(above)*, Google Nexus, Samsung Galaxy Note, Microsoft Surface, Amazon Kindle Fire, and Dell Latitude 10, among others.

Researching the Competition

You may think you have an idea for an app that no one else has thought of but that everyone needs. But before you start creating this app, you need to do your homework. With more than a million-and-a-half apps already available, your great idea might already exist. Of course, you can create an app that is similar to what's already out there, but to be successful you need to offer something those other apps don't. If you can't be the first one to introduce an app, you need to develop the best app of the bunch. Study the competition to find out what the current apps are lacking or if there is a way to improve on what's already available.

Pricing Your App

If you want to make a profit, you need to sell your app. Deciding how much to sell it for can be challenging. The decision depends, in part, on which operating system—Apple iOS or Google Android—you decide to design your app for. For example, for apps sold at the Apple App Store, Apple keeps about one-third of the asking price. So you will earn about $2 per sale if you price your app for $2.99. If you developed the app yourself, then you get to keep all the profit. But if you paid a developer $2,000 to help create your app, you won't begin turning a profit until you've made back what you've spent to develop the app. In this case, you'll need to sell one thousand apps before you begin to make a profit.

Apps can run on both tablets and smartphones. The Facebook app, for example, allows you to update your status and post photos via your phone or tablet from any location.

Promoting Your App

With hundreds of thousands of apps out there, how will anyone know where to look for your app, assuming they even know that it exists at all? You need to find a way to stand out from the crowd and get noticed.

File   Edit   View   Favorites   Tools   Help

STRATEGIES FOR DESIGNING SUCCESSFUL APPS

Strategies for Designing Successful Apps

- **Be engaging:** An app should do something cool or draw the user's attention in a unique and engaging way. A user should want to tell his or her friends about it and encourage them to buy it.

- **Put the user first:** The app isn't for the developer. It's for the user. As you develop an app, take steps to ensure that you anticipate the users' needs and that you care about their interests. Make it easy and intuitive to use.

- **Be unusual, but substantive:** With hundreds of thousands of apps available, if you don't do something interesting, unusual, or unique, or provide quality content in a surprising way, your app will be overlooked.

- **Hide your interface:** You need to show your users only what matters and keep the complicated programming stuff hidden. Make sure that what's relevant for the app is easy to find and that the "architecture" and mechanics of the app remain behind the scenes.

- **Good apps are extendible:** The last thing you want to create is an app that has one and only one use. A strong, versatile app can live on through in-app purchases, connections to online versions, and other services.

Using social networking sites like Facebook and Twitter to alert family and friends of your app will help. Think of other ways you can promote your app so that people will want to seek it out and buy it.

Choosing a Platform

Right now there are two main platforms for which developers create apps. Many popular apps are created to run on multiple platforms, which means they can reach more users (rather than Apple users only, for example). Users download the version of the app they need for their particular device.

Apple products all use the iOS operating system. This operating system cannot be installed on non-Apple products, therefore apps created for

Boarding passes   **Store cards**   **Movie tickets**

Apps now enable access to information, tools, and services such as virtual boarding passes, credit cards and store coupon codes, movie tickets, shopping lists, and more. Apps make your phone an at-your-fingertips resource for anything and everything you might need.

Apple products cannot be downloaded to non-Apple products. Many non-Apple products use Android, an operating system designed primarily for touchscreen mobile devices like smartphones and tablets. Android and iOS are the two main platforms. Even though others, like the Blackberry OS operating system used by Blackberry products, exist, they are not widely used for app development.

Understanding the Language

Web apps are built using software programs such as HTML, CSS, and other programming languages designed specifically for creating Web sites and Web-based projects.

What Is HTML?

HTML stands for hypertext markup language. It's the main language used to mark up text for display on Web pages and other information that can be displayed in a Web browser. Programmers use HTML tags to define how they want text to look. HTML tags can be used to make text bold, italicized, or underlined. They can also establish headers and subheads and indicate when a paragraph should begin and end. For advanced programmers, HTML can be used to create elaborate charts, to hide text on Web pages, and to create lists.

What Is CSS?

CSS is short for Cascading Style Sheets, a programming language that describes the look and formatting of a document written in a markup language, such as HTML. A style sheet is a set of rules that include font, size, colors, and layout that are decided by the programmer. CSS is commonly used to style Web pages written in HTML. Programmers can decide how they want to design the content of a Web page and create

```
backg
(window).resi
        backgroundmoveTo
})
   // ajax trigger for history back
window.onpopstate = function(e) {
        if(e.state){
           console.log(e)
           var objid = e.state.obji
           if($("#"+objid).length)
                $("#"+objid).trigge
        }else {
           var $lasta = null;
           $("a").each(functi
              (e.state.ob
```

Web apps are built using software programs and programming languages that were designed specifically for creating Web sites and Web-based projects. Above is a sample of code written in JavaScript, a common programming language.

a cascading style sheet so that there is stylistic consistency throughout that page.

What Is JavaScript?

JavaScript is a scripting language commonly implemented as part of a Web browser in order to create enhanced user interfaces and dynamic Web sites. For mobile apps, which direct users to a Web site, this program can help a developer design a more engaging experience when users visit the site from a smartphone or tablet.

Chapter 3

The Role of Developers

Paul Dunahoo runs a small company called Bread and Butter Software LLC. Among many other business trips, he was recently invited to attend Apple's prestigious Worldwide Developer Conference in San Francisco, California, to meet other developers and to submit his work for critique. While he is best known for creating the first note-taking app, called Scrawl, Dunahoo faces a unique challenge most other chief executive officers (CEOs) don't. He balances the running of his company with attendance at middle school. Dunahoo is only thirteen years old.

Apple has reported that for the last several years it has received e-mails from teenage developers who have already launched several apps and who are interested in attending the Worldwide Developer Conference. These teens represent a growing group of developers who spend their free time learning how to develop apps. Because they are launching such exciting and popular apps, Apple has extended an invitation to some of these teen developers to take part in the conference.

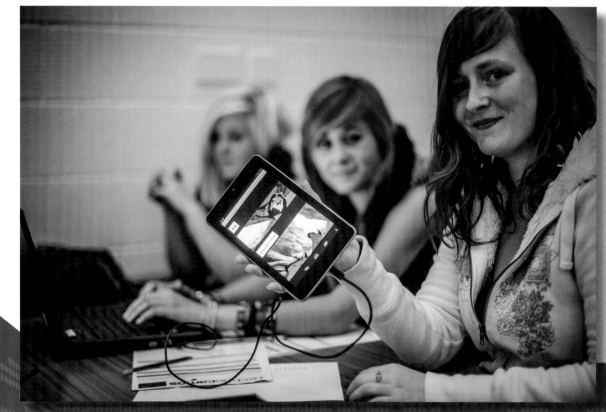

A growing group of developers are teenagers who have taught themselves programming languages and have created apps. Conferences and workshops are now available for teens to learn more about developing, game design, app development, and artificial intelligence.

What Is a Developer?

Developers work with multiple programming languages and with several different operating systems to create apps and new software, and to program and design Web sites. One of the most fascinating parts of their job is to develop new and innovative apps for computers, mobile phones, tablets, and other types of electronic devices. Developers are employed by major technology companies, such as Google, Apple, and Intel. Some developers work independently, however, and instead sell their work to these major companies.

Educational Requirements

Many developers have a college degree in computer science, software engineering, or another related field such as information technology. These college-level degree programs provide knowledge of operating systems, computer networks, and computer theory. They also include courses in various programming languages, computer security, computer graphics, interactive entertainment, usability, artificial intelligence, and data and information management.

Some developers are self-taught and learn programming and developing skills on their own. For teens, there are summer programs, such as the iD Tech Camps. At these camps students learn programming, how to build apps, the design and development of Web sites, and other computer and Web-based tech skills. Regardless of which route they take, developers need to master certain skills. These include:

- **Interface design:** These skills help you create an app that is easy and engaging for the user.
- **Computing knowledge:** Helpful computer skills include database management, security, and hardware interaction.
- **Programming languages:** Common programming languages include object-oriented languages (Java, C++), Web development languages (HTML, CSS), and cross-platform software (Antenna, AMP).

There are several software packages that enable developers to learn how to create apps without any type of formal education. These include:

- **Apple Xcode:** Apple Xcode is a package of tools that provides a user with everything he or she needs to create apps for iPhones and iPads.
- **buzztouch:** buzztouch is Web-based software that includes multiple tools used to design and create apps for both the iOS and

Young developers have access to software packages that can help them build apps. For those who are interested in becoming professional developers, college programs that include course work in interface design, programming languages, database management, computer security, networking and system administration, and information security will be key.

Android operating systems. The software also helps the user manage content used in the apps.

- **Android App Inventor:** The App Inventor, created by Google but now managed by the Massachusetts Institute of Technology (MIT), helps users create apps for the Android operating system.

How Developers Make Money

Coming up with an innovative idea and then putting in the hard work to program, construct, test, and refine the app are only part of the process of developing a successful app. Selling the app and making money are the next crucial stages in the process. App developers can make money by creating and

File   Edit   View   Favorites   Tools   Help

THE SUCCESS OF ANGRY BIRDS

The Success of *Angry Birds*

Angry Birds has become one of the most downloaded games in history. The game, which involves a slingshot used to shoot birds at pigs hiding in various structures, is easy to use, entertaining, and engaging. The goal is to kill as many pigs as possible, using the fewest birds with the greatest accuracy. The game was designed for mobile phones and tablets and is available on both the iOS and Android operating systems.

To date, the game has been downloaded more than 648 million times. There are multiple versions of the game, each of which must be purchased separately. These versions include *Angry Birds Rio*, *Angry Birds Star Wars*, *Angry Birds Magic*, *Angry Birds Space*, and *Angry Birds Seasons*. Each version includes new graphics, such as *Star Wars*–themed characters, and new gameplay mechanics. Worldwide, *Angry Birds* players spend roughly two hundred million minutes a day playing versions of the game.

selling apps, but the amount of money you make depends on a lot of factors, including how popular your app is, what platform it was designed for, where it's made available or sold, and how many people buy your app. Apps are big business and can make a lot of money for both the developer and the store that hosts them. Apple currently offers more than 800,000 apps for the iPhone and iPad. More than 25 billion apps have been downloaded to date. The Apple App Store generates nearly $5.4 million in sales per day for the 200 top-selling apps. Google offers roughly 500,000 apps, and 10 billion have been downloaded. Google generates $679,000 a day for its top 200 apps.

Developers make money off the sale of their apps. Both Apple and Google, which owns the Android operating system, give developers 70

Angry Birds is one of the most popular game apps of all time, with more than 648 million downloads. Mighty Eagle *(left)* and Henri Holm, executives at Rovio, the company behind *Angry Birds*, are planning on opening theme parks and stores around the world based on the game and its characters.

percent of the price of each app sold. If you sell your app for 99 cents, you will make 69 cents every time that APP is purchased. That may not seem like a lot of profit, but think about the top-selling apps. *Angry Birds* is one of the most popular gaming apps. It sells for just 99 cents per download. At last count, *Angry Birds* has sold 648 million downloads worldwide. The developers (or in this case, Rovio, the company that owns *Angry Birds*) are making millions of dollars a day.

When it comes to app sales, the big money is in creating games. If you want to profit from app development, your best bet is to develop a game. They are the most profitable and the most popular type of app downloaded.

TEN GREAT QUESTIONS

TO ASK AN APP DEVELOPER

1 What was the last app you created that you think is great, and why?

2 What kind of phone or tablet do you use, and what are your favorite apps?

3 Is it better to work for a company or independently?

4 I want my app to look really cool. Do I need to learn design skills to be a developer?

5 What are the pros and cons of developing an app by doing all the programming yourself versus using app software like the Android App Inventor or Apple Xcode?

6 Which platform (Apple iOS or Android) do you like best, and why?

7 You always hear these amazing stories about developers who have made a lot of money off of one app. Is that realistic or typical? How much money does the typical developer make for each app he or she has designed?

8 What's a typical day like for an app developer?

9 What's the best piece of advice you have for someone who wants to learn to build apps?

10 What are the most important skills I need as an app developer?

Chapter 4

Building a Better App

If successful apps were easy to create, then every app would enjoy the level of runaway, out-of-nowhere success that *Angry Birds* has. But the reality is that building a successful app is hard work. It takes a great idea; lots of time; long hours of nose-to-the-grindstone programming, testing, and refining; and more than a little luck.

How to Build a Successful App

You can improve your chances of building a successful app by following a few rules. These guidelines give you a chance to create an app that has an opportunity to be successful.

- **Don't rush the development process.** You might have a great idea, but you can rush the development process by skipping important steps. You can't build a house without a blueprint. In the same way, you can't create an app without knowing what it will do, how you will make it do what you want it to do, who it is for, how they will use it, and on what platform.

Coming up with an idea for an app might be the easy part. Developers must spend time testing the app to make sure it works smoothly, thinking about the user experience and marketing it so that it sells.

- **Test, test, and retest your app.** Once your app is done, you're not really finished. You need to test your app for bugs and problems. Even small issues can frustrate people and keep them from using and recommending your app.
- **Think about the user.** Your app should be simple to use and easy to access. If you have extra buttons or if it takes users more than one step to get to where they want to go, you run the risk of them dumping your app in frustration.

- **Avoid "feature creep."** "Feature creep" refers to unnecessary functions or features in your app. These might seem cool to you, but successful apps are designed with a specific, tightly focused, and limited set of purposes in mind. When you add unnecessary features, you weaken the app's chances for utility, popularity, and success.
- **Create a devoted following.** Add features to your app that no one else has. Make it customizable by the user and intuitive.
- **Focus on the small details.** Every design element must be evaluated for its usefulness. A certain design element might look cool, but if it slows down the speed of the app or lessens its functionality, then it might need to be eliminated.

Many app developers work on teams that have members who are experts in certain aspects of the app development process. This allows developers to focus on the app's function, while designers can spend time on the look of the app. Meanwhile, business and marketing specialists can decide how best to market the app and make money.

- **Continue to make improvements.** Listen to feedback and ask outside developers to test your app. You might have missed a solution or a feature because you're too close to the project. Outside opinions can help you see things you might have missed.

Should You Hire a Developer or Do It Yourself?

If you have an interest in computer programming or software engineering, you can, with some trial and error, probably build an app all by yourself. There are several good reference books available, as well as conferences

There are pros and cons to doing the work yourself versus hiring a developer. If you hire a professional developer, you'll get someone who is immersed in the world of apps and can help bring your idea to life. If you decide to create the app yourself, there could be a steep learning curve as you learn more about developing, programming languages, and the business side of apps.

that can provide you with some of the insider tips and techniques that will make the work easier and more successful. In addition, if you take courses in programming and use one of the tool sets available for inexperienced developers, such as Xcode or App Inventor, you can learn even more tricks of the trade.

But what if you're not tech-savvy? What if you have a great idea for an app, but you have little interest in understanding the programming aspect of the process? In this case, you can hire a developer to help you create your app.

There are individual developers whom you can hire and there are entire design and development companies that you can work with who will create an app for you, based on your vision and specifications. Hiring an outside developer costs money, however. The price will depend on how complex the app is, how much work you have already done on the project, and how detailed the design needs to be.

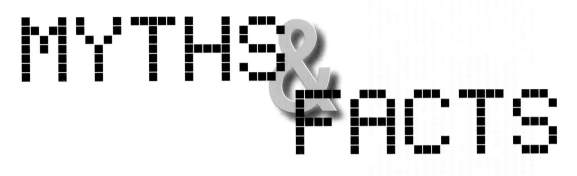

MYTHS & FACTS

MYTH Anyone can create an app if he or she uses Apple Xcode or the Android App Inventor.

FACT While these tools can help you create an app, it may not be the best way to go. Apps created using these types of software tend to all look the same. App stores are full of every kind of app you can imagine. Your app has to set itself apart from the crowd, and looking like every other app won't help it do that.

MYTH Apps are expensive to create.

FACT Not always. Some experienced developers play around and create apps in their spare time. Other people hire developers to create an app for an idea they come up with. The costs associated with developing an app depend on whether you are a developer skilled in programming and design and can create your own app or you have to hire someone to do the work for you.

MYTH Once I create an app, my job is done.

FACT Creating an app is just the beginning of the process. You have to work to get the app noticed and then promote and sustain its popularity and sales/downloads. You also have to keep revising and improving the app to keep it relevant and popular. For example, *Angry Birds* has multiple versions that all offer a slightly different game experience. After playing the original *Angry Birds* app, many users went and purchased additional alternate versions. This generated a lot of money for *Angry Birds*.

Chapter 5

Selling Your App

The next step in the process of developing your app is selling it and getting it noticed. Competition has driven down the price for most apps to $1.99 or less. This increases the pressure on developers to sell even more apps in order to make a profit. But for any app to make money, customers must be able to find it, like it, and download it.

Where you choose to sell your app depends on the platform you have chosen to support your app. If you designed your app for Google Android devices, you will need to sell your app at Google Play. Apps developed for Apple devices are sold at the Apple App Store. Apps for Blackberry devices are sold at Blackberry App World. If you have designed your app to work on multiple platforms (as *Angry Birds* does), you will want to make it available at all of these stores. Just as each operating system has its pros and cons, so, too, do the corresponding app stores.

The Apple App Store

The Apple App Store is the biggest app store, offering more than eight hundred thousand apps. It features the widest variety, ranging from lifestyle and finance

There are hundreds of thousands of apps available for smartphones and tablet computers with prices that range from 99 cents to more than $10.

to music, games, and educational and entertainment apps. The Apple App Store features both free and moderately priced apps that range from 99 cents to upward of $9.99 each. Apple makes use of iTunes, a media library that enables users to download apps, music, television shows, and movies. No other app store offers users this type of one-stop shopping experience.

There are downsides to using the Apple App Store, however. The Apple App Store and iTunes are the only sites from which users can install apps in their Apple products (iPhone, iPad, iPod). And only the most down-loaded apps are featured prominently on the store's site. So if you are trying to attract attention to your app, it may be difficult at first until word of mouth or your own marketing efforts boost its popularity and number of downloads.

Google Play

Used by Android-based products, Google Play features about five hundred thousand apps. The majority of these apps are offered as free downloads. Each app is categorized and listed in a neat and organized manner.

Many users find that the quality of apps on Google Play is poor. This is because of the nonrestrictive manner in which developers can upload apps to

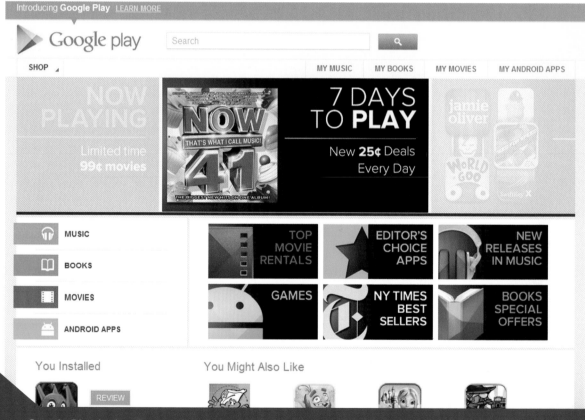

Google Play is the place to download apps and games and buy music, movies, and books for Android-based smartphones and tablets. The site offers more than five hundred thousand apps.

the site. Unlike how Apple oversees its App Store, Google imposes no quality control or approval process upon apps uploaded to its store. In addition, Google has allowed only twenty-nine countries to sell apps for profit. Developers from other countries can only offer free apps at Google Play. This limits the ability of developers from those countries that are not allowed to sell apps for a profit to make money. It inhibits their incentive to put much time, money, or effort into the development of new, exciting, and innovative apps.

Blackberry App World

For Blackberry products, apps are sold at Blackberry App World. Because Apple and Android devices are so much more popular, however, there

Once downloaded, apps sit on your smartphone or tablet's desktop, where they can easily be launched with the touch of a finger.

are relatively few apps designed for Blackberry and available at its store. However, developers stand to make the most money per sale with Blackberry, as they are allowed to collect 80 percent of the sale price of the app.

Apps tend to be more expensive on Blackberry's site, primarily because it sells comparatively few apps. In order to maintain a decent profit margin with smaller sales numbers, it must offer each app at a higher price. This, however, tends to dampen users' enthusiasm and may result in even fewer sales. Users may even switch to Apple or Android products. In addition, some Blackberry customers complain of problems during app installation, and access to the site is limited to only certain countries. Blackberry also requires developers to pay up to $200 to register an account with the store. This is by far the highest fee of any app store.

| File | Edit | View | Favorites | Tools | Help |

ISHOOT: AN OVERNIGHT SUCCESS

iShoot: **An Overnight Success**

Ethan Nicholas worked full-time at Sun Microsystems. In his spare time, however, he began to develop an app called *iShoot*, a game in which the user operates a tank and blasts enemy tanks with a range of high-powered weapons. As tanks blow up, the landscape is automatically rearranged.

Nicholas uploaded the game to the Apple App Store and offered it for sale at $2.99 per download. Feedback from iPhone ranked it as "just OK." So over a holiday break, Nicholas worked on improving the game. He then released a free, lite version of the game to advertise the new and improved version that could be downloaded for a price. Ten days later, the improved *iShoot* app became the number one paid app in the iTunes App Store, with 16,972 downloads in a single day. By releasing a free, lite version, Nicholas gave gamers a chance to play the game without having to buy it and see if they liked the improvements he had made.

Just because your app is ready to be sold, it doesn't mean it'll be accepted by a store for sale. While Google Play does not have an approval process, the Apple App Store does. Apple retains the right to reject your application for sale or to pull your app from the store for no stated reason. While this may seem harsh, apps sold at the Apple App Store all meet a minimum level of quality, and this ensures a mostly positive experience for users.

Market Your App

Here are some tips and tricks to use to help market your app and get it noticed:

- **Build a great app.** This goes without saying, but you need a great app if you're going to get people to download and use it. Make your app easy to use, creative, innovative, fun, and something people need. A great app helps people complete everyday activities quickly and easily, entertains, informs, and simply delights (or all of these things at once). In short, a great app makes daily life easier and/or more pleasurable.
- **Design lite and paid versions.** A lite version of your app, which is usually free, is like a sneak peek at what the fully functioning, paid version can do. Some users who are curious about your app but unwilling to commit or who wonder if they will truly make use of it will sometimes download the lite version to try it out. If they like it, they'll buy the paid version. Having both versions gives you a chance to reach more people and gain some exposure for your app.
- **Spend money on ads.** Paid advertising is an easy way to get your app noticed. Choose sites visited and viewed by the type of people who are most likely to be intrigued by and download your app.
- **Get free exposure.** Free publicity is great if you can get it. To help get the word out about your app, contact Web sites and bloggers

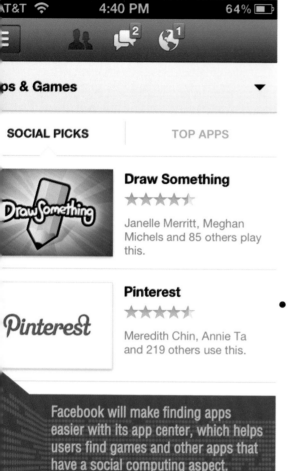

Facebook will make finding apps easier with its app center, which helps users find games and other apps that have a social computing aspect.

who offer reviews of apps and see if they will try out and possibly write about your app. Reviewers will use your app and then write about how it functions, what its purpose is, and how useful it can be to users. Dozens of reviewing Web sites have popped up that offer app users a place to find out about the newest and coolest offerings. Many bloggers and app-oriented Web sites have loyal followers who rely upon their opinions and expertise to learn about the latest must-have apps and newest technologies.

- **Listen to feedback.** When you start getting feedback from users, you need to listen to what they are saying. These are the people who are using your app, and they may have useful and insightful things to say about how it works, its flaws and weaknesses, and how it can be improved. If they pinpoint a problem, check it out and make the necessary adjustments. If you ignore the feedback and don't offer improvements to your app, your sales will almost certainly suffer.

One final tip: go global! Some app developers have reported that nearly 50 percent of their sales come from outside the United States. There's a big world out there and lots of people who have smartphones and tablets. Make sure to cast the widest possible net when seeking users for your new app.

GLOSSARY

browser A computer program used for accessing sites or information on a network, such as the World Wide Web.

bug An unexpected defect or flaw in software.

download To get information off the Internet and save it to a hard drive.

interface The ability for two or more computer systems to communicate with one another.

network A system of computers and databases connected by communication lines.

operating system Software that controls the operation of a computer and directs the running of its programs.

platform Computer equipment that uses a particular operating system.

programming The ability to direct a computer to perform certain tasks.

publicity Attracting attention for someone or something.

scripting language A programming language that tells a computer which tasks to automatically perform without human interaction or commands.

smartphone A cellular phone that includes additional software functions, such as Internet capability.

software A collection of computer programs and related data that provides the instructions for telling a computer what to do and how to do it. Software refers to one or more computer programs and data held in the storage of the computer.

tablet A one-piece mobile computer, primarily operated by touchscreen with an onscreen, hideable virtual keyboard (removing the necessity for a physical keyboard and mouse).

tag To mark something for identification purposes.

usability The ease of use of a human-made object.

Web Short for "World Wide Web," a system of interlinked hypertext documents (Web pages) accessed via the Internet.

Educational Computing Organization of Ontario (ECOO)
10 Morrow Avenue, Suite 202
Toronto, ON M6R 2J1
Canada
(416) 489-1713
Web site: http://www.ecoo.org
The ECOO helps teachers and students incorporate computer learning into
the educational process.

Emagination Computer Camps
54 Stiles Road, Suite 205
Salem, NH 03079
(877) 248-0206
Web site: http://www.computercamps.com
Emagination's programs are designed to enable children to express their
creativity, advance their technology skills, make friends, learn independence, and develop self-confidence.

The Fund for Social Entrepreneurs
Youth Service America (YSA)
1101 15th Street, Suite 200
Washington, DC 20005
Web site: http://www.servenet.org
This organization provides financial support to youth groups interested in
entrepreneurial endeavors.

High Tech Kids
111 Third Avenue South, Suite 145

Minneapolis, MN 55401
(612) 781-2203
Web site: http://www.hightechkids.org
High Tech Kids helps kids discover the fun in science, technology, and computing.

iD Tech Camps
42 West Campbell Avenue, Suite 301
Campbell, CA 95008
(888) 709-8324
Web site: http://www.internaldrive.com
This organization offers summer camps and courses in computing and technology.

International Technology Education Association (ITEA)
1914 Association Drive, Suite 201
Reston, VA 20191-1539
(703) 860-2100
Web site: http://www.iteaconnect.org
The International Technology Education Association promotes technology
    education and literacy.

The Internet Society (ISOC)
1775 Wiehle Avenue, Suite 201
Reston, VA 20190-5108
(703) 439-2120
Web site: http://www.isoc.org
The ISOC is a nonprofit organization that concentrates on maintaining high
    standards for Internet infrastructure and promotes education and govern-
    ment policies that promote open online environments.

Media Smarts
950 Gladstone Avenue, Suite 120
Ottawa, ON K1Y 3E6
Canada
(613) 224-7721
Web site: http://mediasmarts.ca
MediaSmarts is a Canadian not-for-profit charitable organization for digital
and media literacy. Its mission is to provide children and youth with the
critical thinking skills necessary to engage with media as active and
informed digital citizens.

Web Sites

Due to the changing nature of Internet links, Rosen Publishing has developed
an online list of Web sites related to the subject of this book. This site is
updated regularly. Please use this link to access the list:

http://www.rosenlinks.com/DIL/Apps

FOR FURTHER READING

Briggs, Jason R. *Python for Kids: A Playful Introduction to Programming*. San Francisco, CA: No Starch Press, 2012.

Clark, Josh. *Tapworthy: Designing Great iPhone Apps*. Sebastopol, CA: O'Reilly Media, 2010.

Darby, Jason. *Game Creation for Teens*. Independence, KY: Course Technology PTR, 2008.

Farrell, Mary. *Computer Programming for Teens*. Boston, MA: Course Technology PTR, 2007.

Ford, Jerry Lee, Jr. *Scratch Programming for Teens*. Boston, MA: Course Technology PTR, 2008.

Hardnett, Charles. *Programming Like a Pro for Teens*. Boston, MA: Course Technology PTR, 2011.

Miller, Michael. *Absolute Beginner's Guide to Computer Basics*. Indianapolis, IN: Que Publishing, 2007.

Mureta, Chad. *App Empire: Make Money, Have a Life, and Let Technology Work for You*. Hoboken, NJ: Wiley, 2012.

Sande, Warren, and Carter Sande. *Hello World! Computer Programming for Kids and Other Beginners*. Shelter Island, NY: Manning Publications, 2009.

Sethi, Maneesh. *Game Programming for Teens*. Independence, KY: Course Technology PTR, 2008.

White, Ron, and Timothy Downs. *How Computers Work*. Indianapolis, IN: Que Publishing, 2007.

Yarmosh, Ken, and John Jantsch. *App Savvy: Turning Ideas into iPad and iPhone Apps Customers Really Want*. Sebastopol, CA: O'Reilly Media, 2010.

BIBLIOGRAPHY

AppCulture. "Seven Traits of Highly Successful Apps." Retrieved November 2012 (http://appculture.net/the-seven-traits-of-highly-successful-apps).

Gilbert, Jason. "Most Popular Free Apps for iPhone, iPad: Apple Reveals Biggest Downloads of All Time." *Huffington Post*, June 6, 2012. Retrieved November 2012 (http://www.huffingtonpost.com/2012/03/05/most-popular-free-apps-iphone-ipad_n_1321852.html).

Kristof, Kathy. "How to Build an iPhone App in 6 Easy Steps." CBSNews.com, July 7, 2010. Retrieved November 2012 (http://www.cbsnews.com/8301-505144_162-36942435/how-to-build-an-iphone-app-in-6-easy-steps).

Laird, Sam. "So You Want to Be an App Developer? Here's How." Mashable.com, August 28, 2012. Retrieved November 2012 (http://mashable.com/2012/08/28/app-developer-infographic).

Lenox, Brooke. "How to Market iPhone Apps." OnlineMarketingRant.com, May 16, 2009. Retrieved November 2012 (http://www.onlinemarketingrant.com/how-to-market-iphone-apps).

Matzner, Ryan. "Why Web Apps Will Crush Native Apps." Mashable.com, September 12, 2012. Retrieved October 2012 (http://mashable.com/2012/09/12/web-vs-native-apps).

Pierce, Taylor A. *Appreneur: Secrets to Success in the App Store*. Seattle, WA: CreateSpace, 2012.

The Week Editorial Staff. "The Rise of the Teenage App-Developer." *The Week*, June 20, 2012. November 2012 (http://theweek.com/article/index/229474/the-rise-of-the-teenage-app-developer).

Wooldridge, Dave, and Michael Schneider. *The Business of iPhone and iPad App Development: Making and Marketing Apps That Succeed*. New York, NY: Apress, 2011.

INDEX

About the Author

Laura La Bella has written numerous books on technology, science, commerce, business, careers, and Web development. La Bella lives in Rochester, New York, with her husband and son.

Photo Credits

Cover and p. 1 (from left) Andresr/Shutterstock.com, bannosuke /Shutterstock.com, Robert Kneschke/Shutterstock.com, ollyy/Shutterstock. com; p. 4 Rex Features via AP Images; p. 7 Jim Wilson/The New York Times/Redux Pictures; p. 8 altrendo images/Stockbyte/Getty Images; pp. 10, 18, 26 © AP Images; p. 12 Till Jacket/Photononstop/Getty Images; p. 15 Bloomberg/Getty Images; p. 16 © iStockphoto.com/Özgür Donmaz; p. 20 iStockphoto/Thinkstock; p. 22 © Keith Morris/Alamy; p. 24 © redsnapper/Alamy; p. 29 Jacek Chabraszewski/Shutterstock.com; p. 30 Maciej Noskowski/the Agency Collection/Getty Images; p. 31 © iStockphoto.com/David Hills; p. 35 age fotostock/SuperStock; p. 36 AP Images/Google; p. 37 © iStockphoto.com/Norman Chan; p. 40 AP Images/Facebook; cover (background) and interior page graphics © iStock-photo.com/suprun.

Designer: Nicole Russo
Photo Researcher: Karen Huang